ABOUT THE

Markella Mikkelsen received a Ph.D.
many years in the private and public hea ., she decided to
start her own property investment company in the UK in 2008. She
did as she preaches in this book and she is now a successful investor
and entrepreneur with a property portfolio worth over £1 million.

Markella's passion is to inspire other people to succeed in creating the
life of their dreams. Financial freedom to her means devoting her time
to the activities she loves and choses to pursue.

Her vision is to combine her background in Genetics and her entrepre-
neurial skills to help eradicate genetic disease this century.

"This book takes you step-by-step through the maze of how to start your own business. Markella understands first-hand the emotions, challenges, and techniques she had to conquer to set up her own company while holding down a full-time job! If you're determined to achieve success as an entrepreneur through these challenging times and are daunted by the constraints imposed by the time needed for your own business and the fact that you're working full-time to pay the bills then this is the book to get. Markella takes you by the hand and guides you through the real-world situations that you will face, through the shifts in mindset that makes everything else easier, and she helps you actually implement efficient systems so that you can achieve success. And she does all this in an easy-to-understand way"

-RICHARD SHEPHERD,
UK PROPERTY INVESTOR

THE ENTREPRENEUR WITHIN

A step-by-step guide to starting your own business

MARKELLA MIKKELSEN

To Marc
and his two beautiful daughters,
for inspiring me to write this book

Table of Contents

Acknowledgements

First and foremost I want to thank Raymond Aaron and his team. Without his inspiration, hard work and support, I would not be holding this book in my hands today. Thank you, Raymond, for your unstoppable energy.

Several people have been influential in my journey, and I would like to thank them all. I would not be where I am standing today without the help and support of:

Glenn Armstrong, my coach and mentor, who is constantly stretching my mind and expanding my horizons, I am so grateful for what you are teaching me.

Vanish Patel, who four years ago made me write my goals on a piece of paper and set the ball rolling.

Richard Shepherd, for his continued trust and support.

Angela Mendes, my mentor, for teaching me to be a more complete and balanced human being.

Steve Moss, for painstakingly deciphering my recording and providing a transcript of the book.

Sally Nyland, my editor, for her indomitable enthusiasm, her incredible attention to detail and her sense of humour (humor).

Finally, I would like to thank my family for their unconditional love and support and my friends for their loyalty and acceptance of who I am.

1
ORDINARY BEGINNINGS

Have you ever felt that you were stuck in a 9 to 5 rut and you didn't know how to get out? Do you make do with what you've got, but know that you were destined for much more in life? Do you have occasional flashes of what life would be like if you lived it to the fullest? Do you even flounder at the thought of where to start to make changes? If you answered "yes" to any of these questions, this book probably has the answers you've been looking for.

My story will probably touch many of you on the grounds that it sounds familiar. Some of you may be where I started my journey back in 2008, or at some point along the way. If so, when you discover that I was not in such a different place from where you are, and you see how far I've come, perhaps it will give you courage to start your own new journey.

There is nothing extraordinary about my education and my academic abilities. I went to an ordinary school and got ordinary grades. In fact, I was labelled as a bit of a dreamer at school; I found it hard to concentrate on a subject for any length of time. My homework was always done at the last minute, if at all. I did enough to get by and graduate. I somehow sensed that memorising the rules of trigonometry and remembering battle dates were not going to make me any money.

Essentially, I found most subjects vastly removed from reality. Does this sound familiar?

What was drummed into me from an early age was that if you worked hard at school and got good grades, you'd get somewhere. My teachers often repeated, "If you study hard, you will go to University. If you get your University degree, you'll get a job. If you work hard in your job, you'll get a good pension"—things that I know many kids heard when they were at school. I now know plenty of people who did not get good grades at school and have done very well for themselves by using their talent and imagination and putting in the needed work.

Don't get me wrong; I do not want to put down the merits of a conventional education, and this is not a book about not getting a conventional education. On the contrary, you should definitely invest time in getting the best education you can. It's just that what I wished for as a school kid was the choice of having a more balanced education. Unfortunately, the "Make Your Money Work For You" class came much later.

My parents were comfortable, but by no means rich, and money was always an issue. My family had to budget every month as my father was the only wage earner, so we knew that there was a limited amount of money to be had every month. We just had to keep our budget to something quite reasonable. From this, I learned to live within my means, modelling my spending and saving patterns after those of my parents. While this provided me with good money management lessons, it also exposed me to the realities of what one could expect with earnings from a traditional job.

In terms of my "life's journey," the principles of my family reflected those of my teachers—"Get an education, go to University, get a job, get a pension." And so it was inevitable that I would pursue a University degree. I studied genetics and did very well, graduating with a first class honours. While pursuing my degree there was always a little voice in my head saying, "Go to University, get a degree, get a job, get a pension." So throughout my early life, the focus on the importance of a job was always there. Getting a good job was not merely something you fell upon or something that might be a possibility—it was an expectation.

As soon as I graduated, I got a job. My first job was in the National Health Service (NHS), working as a medical scientist. This was considered a very good job—the NHS is a government job; it meant stability with a good pension in the future. I'd made it. Most people would call me fortunate—the path of my career in the public sector had been carved. All I had to do to receive my well-deserved pension was to work for the NHS for the next 40 years. Great, right?

Well, actually, no. I had worked in the health industry for almost 20 years. I had been very successful in my job, reaching the top tiers of my profession, and there had been aspects of my job that I enjoyed very much. But there was always something missing. I kept hearing that little voice, and I started to wonder, "Am I going to work until I am 65, retire with my pension, and then die? Is this it?" As time went on, the little voice became louder. But everything in life was going fairly well, so I kept doing what I was doing. Then life took a twist, and triggered a change.

I had been putting part of my salary into an NHS pension. Why? Because you are told that this is the right thing to do. One day, I received an unexpected letter from the NHS Pensions Department announcing that the first two years of my contributions from an earlier NHS job could no longer be deposited in the fund they were currently invested in, and they were going to be returned to me. What the letter failed to mention was that what was going to be returned to me was going to be taxed handsomely. After having made nearly £5,000 in pension contributions from my own salary for 24 months, I received a cheque in the grand sum of £700. Reality hit—the act of physically holding a cheque for such a measly amount of money got me thinking. How was I going to fund my latter years when I retired? After my divorce, I became solely responsible for my own finances; this was a big deal. Did I really want to spend my life working for the NHS and retire at the age of 65 almost penniless? Could it be that I could put some time and effort into something that would bring financial rewards to me and me alone, bypassing an employer? Following on from that, could it be possible for me to become "financially free" (a term that I didn't know or comprehend at the time) and retire before I turned 65? The little voice was back, but this time, I was starting to think differently; I was starting to take action.

Shortly after this trigger point, I found myself holding in my hand a copy of the book entitled "Rich Dad Poor Dad." I read it from cover to cover in the space of two days. For me, this book acted as an invisible mentor—it changed the way I thought about money, assets and liabilities. It was the first time I heard the term financial freedom—a term that I will use a lot in this book. I had experienced a "light bulb moment."

"Rich Dad Poor Dad" radically changed my thinking. I started thinking outside the box, outside the idea of a salary, a job, a career, a pension. What if I could create some surplus income by starting my own business, and then invest these funds so that in a few years' time these same investments could give me some passive income? And what if I carried on investing so that my passive income could grow steadily and perhaps one day replace my whole salary? What if my passive income could one day overtake my salary so that I could become financially free? Who knows, maybe one day I could become a millionaire! My mind started racing. I wanted to know how I could put these thoughts into action. I was on my way to starting my own business.

At this point, I must tell you that I believe what I experienced did not simply involve coincidence. I believe that when your mind is open to different possibilities and ways of thinking, paths will open up that will help guide you in a new direction, one that is for your best good and one that you may have otherwise passed by.

From the moment I made the decision to start my own business, I've never looked back. I have put in many hours, and there have been some challenges, but I can seriously say that I have not regretted one moment of what I have experienced. I will never look back on my NHS days.

Continue reading this book, because I will show you how you can eliminate all the excuses in your head that have stopped you from making your dreams a tangible reality. I will show you how to take that first step and do exactly what I did without any fear, so that you can live the life you really want, the life that you know you really deserve.

This is not a "Get Rich Quick" book—I don't believe that you can get rich without having a passion, holding a vision, using your imagination and putting in the effort. But if you are prepared to go forward, I will guide you to the other end of the tunnel, where you can see a different life shining through.

Now that we have come to the end of this chapter, I encourage you to go to my website, www.TheEntrepreneurWithinBook.com, and click on Bonus 1 to find out how you can get your hands on "Rich Dad Poor Dad," as well as a list of other books that I strongly recommend.

I look forward to guiding you on this journey.

2

WHY START YOUR OWN BUSINESS?

The Realities of Working in a J.O.B.

I would like to tell you a story.

This story is about a woman called Jane. Jane sets her alarm to wake up every morning at 6:30 a.m. Jane gets up, gets washed and dressed, grabs her bag and walks to the train station. Jane waits on the crowded platform until the train arrives. Sometimes the train arrives on time. Sometimes the train is late. Sometimes the train is cancelled. Regardless, every morning Jane, along with several hundred other people, fights to get on the train. Sometimes she finds a little bit of standing space. Sometimes she is so squashed, she can't even read her book or newspaper. She rarely manages to find a seat, and when she does, she really thinks it's her lucky day. An hour and a half later, Jane gets off the train and makes the 10 minute walk to the office. Upon arrival, she makes herself a cup of coffee, has a little chat with her colleagues to catch up on last night's reality TV programme and then starts working. At 1 o'clock, Jane gets up from her desk and goes out to buy her favourite sandwich. She returns to the office, eats her sandwich, and exchanges a few words with her colleagues before getting back to work. She continues to work until 5:30 p.m. Sometimes her boss expects her to do a little bit extra (for free) so she can't leave until 6:30 p.m. Then she makes the 10 minute walk back to the station. She waits on the platform. Sometimes the train arrives on time. Sometimes the train is late. Sometimes the train has broken down or is cancelled, and she knows she's going to get home late. Once again, with her fellow passengers, she fights her way onto the train. If she's really lucky, she'll find a seat. If not, she'll stand all the way. An hour and a half later, she gets off and walks home. It's now 8 p.m. As soon as she gets home, she throws off her shoes, changes her clothes and turns on the television—her favourite programmes will be coming on soon. While she's watching the latest disaster on the news, she pops a pre-packaged meal into the microwave. She takes the meal out of the microwave and eats it while the news finishes up. Then it's time for an evening of television. At about 11 p.m., Jane's had enough of that. She is now too tired to open her mail or order some book from Amazon that her friend recommended called "Rich Dad Poor Dad." She's been meaning to order that book for three months now (or has it been four?), so it can wait another night. And so off to bed she goes. The End.

Does this story strike a chord with you? Does this sound familiar? Do you know a Jane? Are YOU Jane?

So what is the reality of having a regular, so-called stable job?

You are stuck in a daily routine like millions around the world. Like Jane, you wake up early in the morning, you get in your car, or take a train or bus, and you travel for an hour (or more) to get to work. You work for eight or nine hours, or however long your employer tells you to, and you take the same journey back home. You get back home at 7 p.m. or 8 p.m. at night, have something for dinner, watch the television, and then go to bed. You repeat this process five times a week, four weeks a month, collecting a regular pay cheque. The only time you have for yourself is your weekends. It may be all you really have to look forward to.

Do you get the "Sunday blues," dreading that Monday is just around the corner? Do you count the working days to Friday? Are you counting the days until your next holiday? If so, isn't that wishing your life away? Wouldn't you want to wake up in the morning knowing that you are about to do something that you love doing? Wouldn't you not want to care that it's Sunday morning or Monday morning, because every day is an absolute delight? Now, maybe you are one of those people who are happy with what you've got. If you are, that's absolutely fine—this book is perhaps not for you. But maybe you're saying, "There's more to this life—I can have more in my life than just this job."

At this point, you're probably saying, "This sounds interesting, but I like the security of a regular pay cheque." So, let's look at this reality. You probably work in an office, perhaps alone but most likely on a team, and you have a boss. You generally do as your boss tells you. Maybe you're one of the lucky ones who has a little flexibility in terms of your hours or what you're allowed to do. Maybe you even have a little input regarding what the team does. But essentially you do as your boss tells you, because if you don't, you will lose your job. And at the end of the week or month, you get paid.

Maybe, just maybe you're one of those people who are very happy with their salary, and you have plenty of funds left over at the end of the month. The reality, however, is that the spending pattern of most people follows that of their earning pattern. This means that at the end of the month, you have spent what you've earned. In fact, for most people, at the end of the month spending has exceeded earnings. Does this sound familiar? Do you find yourself counting the days to your next pay cheque because there's a bit more month than there is money? That is the definition of a job, or should I say J.O.B. – Just Over Broke. This is the reality of the regular pay cheque.

"But when I retire, I'll get a pension." Let's look at that reality of having a J.O.B. with a pension. Weeks go by, months go by, years go by with you working Monday to Friday. You have your weekends as well as your vacation time. And at the end of your working years, as many as 45 years, you will have a pension. We are conditioned to think that this is the best course of action for our working life. But I ask you this: How do you know if your pension will be enough to cover the last years of your life? And if right now there is too much month left after you have received your regular pay for the month, how much month will be left when you are dependent on a fixed pension with no opportunities for bonuses or salary increases? Do you want to be penny-pinching for the last years of your life? Is this the lifestyle that you want at the end of your working career? Or would you rather have a life of abundance, a life of wealth to be rewarded for all the years of hard work that you have put in? If this sounds more appealing, then you're reading the right book.

And now you probably hear a little voice inside your head that's saying, "But that's what everyone else does." That's right. Every day, people wake up early, go to work, come home, watch television, and then go to bed. Millions of people do this. It's called a rat race, and you are part of it. If you don't find a way out, this is how your life will be mapped out until you retire. So let's stop for a moment and think. Yes, it's natural for you to hear that voice saying, "But that's what everyone else does."

But is that what you really want to do? Are you starting to wish there could be a way out of the rat race—a different way of doing things? Think about how your life will be from now until the day you retire if you do nothing. Consider that essentially every day of your life will be the same. If you carry on reading this book, I will show you that by starting your own business, by doing it well and doing it properly, there can be a way out. There can be a different, better life.

3

"BUT... I HAVE NO MONEY."

How to Get Rid of the "No Money" Excuse

So why start your own business?

In the previous chapter, we looked at how staying where you are now is going to bring you more of the same. We looked at how clinging on to the so-called stability of a pay cheque and a pension keeps you in the rat race along with everyone else.

How can you get out of the rat race and move toward the life you really want to live? Reflecting on what I have addressed previously—about the realities of having a 9 to 5 job—the truth is:

While you are working for someone else you will NEVER, EVER attain financial freedom.

Being financially free means having enough resources to live the life of your dreams. The only way you will ever be wealthy enough to achieve financial freedom is to have your own business so you are no longer reliant on someone else paying you. So, if this opportunity is so great, why haven't most people jumped at the chance to start their own business? In my experience, there are always the same five obstacles, which come under the guise of an excuse, that prevent people from giving it a go. Each stems from fear—whether resonating from an inner voice or originating from beliefs that have been instilled.

THESE FIVE EXCUSES ARE:

- I have no money.

- I have no time.

- I don't know anything about starting my own business (i.e., I have no knowledge).

- What will my family/friends think of me?

- What if I fail?

Do any of these look familiar? Perhaps you've already used some of them to avoid starting a business of your own. Don't be discouraged, because in the next few chapters we're going to explore these five excuses in depth. I'm going to take each of them, one by one, and I'm going to show you how you can stop the excuses, remove the obstacles, and move toward a richer financial life.

THE #1 EXCUSE

"I have no money." Have you ever used that excuse before? It's one of the most common excuses that people use to stay locked in a J.O.B. I know what you're thinking—to start your own business you need money. And if you're locked in a J. O. B.—that's right, Just Over Broke—it means "more month than money."

Yes, a business needs money to thrive and grow. Cash is the lifeline of every business. But you don't have to let this excuse stop you from moving forward. The good news is that there are imaginative ways of finding money to get your business started.

I am going to show you some ways to generate cash. But first, I want to remind you that this is not a "Get Rich Quick" book. I didn't say this was going to be effortless, and I didn't say this was going to be without sacrifices. If you ask people who are financially free, and didn't inherit their money from rich relatives, they will tell you that they've had to work hard to achieve their dreams. Most likely you'll have to do the same. But there's a rich reward at the end of this process. All your efforts will be worthwhile, believe me.

WHERE TO START

You can actually start to generate some cash by planning a monthly budget. This is a very simple thing to do. Take one or two of your most recent bank statements, and look carefully at every single item on them. Categorize the expenses so you can really see where you're spending money. Then I want you to take that list and split it into two separate ones:

- A list of all the items that you absolutely must have money for each month. There is no way that you could survive without the funds to cover these particular expenses. So the items that would go on this list are things like your mortgage, your electricity and gas bill, any council (property) tax, phone, transportation, and the like. For every item that you put on this list, ask yourself, "Do I really need this?" or "What would happen if I stopped paying for this?" For some items—mortgage/rent, gas bill—the answer will be obvious.

- Look at how much you're spending on food. Write down a reasonable amount, enough so that you certainly do not go hungry, and stick to that amount! This is a time to be really honest with yourself. I am not expecting you to live the life of a martyr—you would eventually rebel and not achieve anything. Neither am I expecting you to starve or buy the cheapest items. This would only train your mind to expect to have the lowest quality of everything.

- A list of all the items that could be considered non-essentials. For these you'd say, "Well, it's nice to have them, but I can survive without them. They are not really necessary." Some examples would be meals out at restaurants, how much you'd spend on new clothes or a new car, or for new gadgets, cigarettes or drinks "down the pub."

To help you with this process, I am giving you a table that includes the two different lists. I want you to fill in this table and really be honest with yourself. How many of your expenses are absolutely necessary? How many are the type to which you'd say, "Well, perhaps I could go down to the pub fewer times a month," or "I could do without this brand new gadget," or maybe "I'll just take one holiday this year." Initially you may feel that you are having to make some sacrifices, but it won't be forever. Remember—doing what you are doing now, spending money the way you spend it now, will keep you in the same position you are now. Focus on the long term benefits—the rewards are going to be tremendous.

Now, just add up the figures on each list. Your first list, the absolute necessities, represents your fixed monthly expenses. This is the minimum amount of money that you need in order to survive. This is your "monthly outgoing.

Now add up the figures on second list. This is what you can save every month! What if it is only £100? That's not trivial. This means that at the end of one year, £1,200 will have been put aside for your future!

MONTHLY EXPENSES			
Absolute Essentials	Amount	Non-Essentials	Amount
Mortgage/Rent Electricity bill Gas bill Water bill Council (property) tax Telephone/Broadband Transportation Food		Restaurant meals Takeaway meals New clothes New gadgets Weekend away Cigarettes Alcohol	
	Total		Total
	Monthly Outgoing		Potential Savings

These lists are representative of typical expenses and are not exhaustive. You are encouraged to customize your expense lists as appropriate to your budget.

WHAT'S NEXT?

Look at the amount of money you have determined that you can save. Make a conscious decision now to open a separate bank account, and put that amount into it at the beginning of every month. By taking this step and following this process, what you will be doing is paying your-self first. Consider the total in the bottom right-hand column as your salary to yourself. It is your seed capital, what you can put toward your future. This is what is eventually going to make you financially free. So, be absolutely disciplined; take that money before you spend it, and put it in a separate bank account. This is one of the most important lessons that I learned when starting my own business. Pay yourself first.

At the end of this chapter, go to my website, www.TheEntrepreneur WithinBook.com. Click on Bonus 2, where you will find this form as a PDF that you can print out and fill in. I urge you to do this as soon as you have finished reading this chapter.

EQUITY FROM PROPERTY

Are you a property owner? If so, look at your current mortgage statement. Is there any equity in your property? There's an easy way to find out. Speak to your lender, your building society or your mortgage broker, and see how much equity you can take out of your house.

This is where I need to give you a little warning. If you share your intentions with your friends, relatives or partner, prepare yourself for a lot of negative feedback. They will turn around and say, "You're risking your house." Well, yes, there is some risk, but it's a calculated risk. Your mortgage broker will tell you how much you can borrow, given your current financial situation and your business plans. This will help you not to overextend yourself. This is the strategy I used to start my business. Let me share my own personal example.

I decided to start a property business in 2008. I had only been a property owner myself for two years but I had equity in my home. At this time, the property market in the UK was already beginning to crash. You can imagine how sceptical my friends were, not only with my desire to start this type of business, but also with my idea of taking equity out of my recently acquired home. Nonetheless, I took £17,000 from the equity that had accrued and made my first investment purchase. This amount was not huge, but it was enough to get my business started, and 3 years later, I found myself the owner of an investment property portfolio worth more than £1 million. The £17,000 is still in my business account, so I do not regret the small, educated risk that I took.

SPEAK TO FAMILY

Is it possible that you have some relatives to whom you might speak about lending you money to start your own business? Yes, there could be a lot of negativity, but perhaps you know someone who is a little bit more open-minded, and would appreciate your plans.

When approaching a relative, be as prepared as you can be. Show him or her a proper business plan. Adopt the manners of a serious business person from the start. Explain exactly what your business is about, who your prospective clients are, how much money you need and exactly what you will do with the money. If you are prepared and you show that you have done your homework, they will trust you.

Even if they can only lend you £5,000 or £10,000, that would be a good starting amount. You could use it to further educate yourself about the field of business you've chosen, or buy needed equipment or supplies. This would be a small but very important start.

So, speak to your relatives, and see if someone will listen carefully to what you have to say. And don't pre-judge. You never know how people might react to your plans. Some may be negative, but some people may be very encouraging. Don't be shy—just try.

One of the most important personal qualities to cultivate when starting a business is tenacity. Do not give up if the first person says "no." Believe that every "no" will get you closer to a "yes."

START A JOINT BUSINESS

Another option is to start your business with a friend or acquaintance. Do you know someone who may have cash available to invest? Perhaps that someone has either been too busy to start a business or doesn't really want to start one, but would like to see his or her money accrue. Speak to that person the same as you would speak to your relatives. Explain exactly what you want to do. Present a business plan. Decide upfront exactly how your friend's money is going to be used, who will be responsible for what, and how the profits are going to be shared. If you're serious about this business opportunity, your friend will be seriously interested. If you are passionate about your business, your friend will become passionate about it. Once again, you could be very surprised by the reaction of some of your friends.

USE CASH FROM CREDIT CARDS

If you have credit cards, preferably those with little or no debt on them, you can actually use cash advances to get start-up money for your business. At this point I would like to be clear that this is a strategy you should use with caution. There's a good reason to use this strategy, but it has a drawback. The good thing is that credit cards provide a ready source of cash that you can put to good use. The down side is that if you are not very careful in paying the advance back, you could end up with more debt than you started.

Here's an example of how I manage cash from credit cards. I have used credit cards to pay for repairs and renovation works on recently purchased properties because cash is usually needed for the work to start. I plan well in advance and know exactly how to manage the payments. Once I have tenants in the property, the rent money goes to repay the credit card debt.

I have also found another good strategy to help manage credit card debt. You can transfer the amount you owe to a 0% interest credit card. These offers are around all the time. You can contact your credit card company and check to see if one is available. With these offers, I pay only an initial transfer fee and then, with very careful planning, I repay the entire balance by the time the 0% interest period is finished.

As you can see, you have to be extremely organised in order to make sure the payments are made on time, otherwise you could get into a lot of debt. The last thing you want is to be overdrawn on your credit cards and in more debt than when you started, so use this strategy with very careful planning and a lot of caution.

The ideas I have shared here are specific and easy to understand, and they will help you find an initial "pot of gold" to start your business. Maybe you can come up with more ideas—be creative! But I don't want to hear, "I have no money." If you really want to be financially free, you will find a way to eliminate this excuse and move forward.

4

"BUT ... I HAVE NO TIME."

How to Use Your Time More Effectively

"How can I start my own business? I have no time." "I don't even have enough hours in the day to do what I already need to do." These are excuses that I often hear. Have you found yourself saying the same thing? Have you ever thought about multi-millionaires and billionaires like Richard Branson, Donald Trump and Warren Buffet? They also have 24 hours a day, yet somehow they find the time to work on their businesses.

In this chapter, I will give you ideas to help you find time to start your own business. It doesn't have to be much. You will see that it is possible to find two to three hours every day to devote to your business even if you have a full-time job. Wouldn't you be willing to set aside that small amount of time to pursue financial freedom? After all, it's your own business that will make you financially free.

HOW ARE YOU SPENDING YOUR DAY?

The first thing I urge you to do is to look at where you're currently spending time. Think about what you do each day. Then take a blank sheet of paper and, for the next 30 minutes, write down all your daily activities and how much time you spend on them. Just as you did with your expenses, make two lists. On one, write down the activities that relate to your daytime job (e.g., commuting, working at the office, etc.). This is time that you cannot devote to starting your business. On the other list, write down those activities that are not related to your job or essential to your daily living. How much time do you spend in front of the TV? How much time do you spend at the pub? How much time do you spend surfing the internet? Once again, I'm providing you with a table to help you with this exercise.

ACTIVITY/TIME ANALYSIS				
A	B	C	D	E
Daytime Job & Essential Activities	Time Spent Daily	Non-Work & Non-Essential Activities	Time Spent Daily	Time Spent Monthly (D x 30)
Commuting Working in the office Sleeping Eating Shopping		Watching TV Meeting friends Surfing the internet Hobbies Shopping		
			Total Hours	Total Hours

These lists are representative of typical activities and are not exhaustive. You are encouraged to customize your activity lists as appropriate.

Add the hours that you spend daily on non-work/non-essential activities (column D) and convert this figure to a monthly figure (column

E). Could you possibly borrow time from these activities to devote to your business?

A PDF version of this form is available for you to print out and fill in. Go to my website, www.TheEntrepreneurWithinBook.com, and click on Bonus 3. I urge you to do this as soon as you have finished reading this chapter.

IDENTIFY TIME KILLERS

Look at the activities that you wrote down that are NOT related to your daytime job. Which ones could you do without on a daily basis? Let's take watching TV as an example. Consider the time you spend in front of the TV each day. Let's say that you average 2 hours per day in front of the box. That translates to 14 hours per week. Multiply this by 52 weeks and, by making this small change, you'd have 728 hours per year available to devote to your business. And I'm being very conservative here—I suspect that your "TV time" is more than 2 hours a day, especially on the weekends. Makes you think, doesn't it?

I can hear some of you saying, "But I want to watch my favourite soap." "I want to watch the news." You certainly can do these—but what has your favourite soap taught you in the past? What is it teaching you now? How are you moving forward toward a richer financial life by watching your favourite soap or a movie for the 2nd, 3rd or possibly 4th time? Wouldn't you enjoy reading a motivational book or attending a seminar or networking event in an area that you're passionate about? Wouldn't that teach you more about your business?

Yes, OK, maybe you'd have to miss your favourite soap, but the reward is that you'll be on your way to financial freedom. And trust me, once the excitement over what you're learning and the progress you're making starts to build, you'll find that you won't miss your old TV habits.

Remember—if you continue to spend your time the way you do now, you will stay in the place you are now.

GET UP ONE HOUR EARLIER

This is a tip I picked up from one of my colleagues. You can always find an extra hour per day by simply waking up an hour earlier. At first, this might sound brutal, but you can make it less painful by making the change in phases. Start by rising 15 minutes earlier for a week or two. After you are used to that, set a new wake-up time—15 minutes earlier. Repeat this process until you find yourself getting up a full hour earlier than you used to. If you are absolutely determined to find the time to start your own business, this is a great idea to help you in that effort.

I find early morning to be a very peaceful and productive time. It's quiet in the house, and I can actually achieve a number of things. Working with a list of "to do" items that I have written the night before, I use this undistracted time to accomplish most of the tasks on that list. It's a great feeling to know that you've made progress on your new business even before starting your daytime job.

WORK ONE OR TWO WEEKENDS OUT OF FOUR

Think about how you spend your time on the weekends. While no one expects you to give up your life for your new business, couldn't you find two to three hours on a weekend to devote to it? Start a new habit of working on your business one weekend a month, then build to two.

If there are family concerns, perhaps you could come to an arrangement with your partner to look after the family or manage the household chores while you focus on your business. Then you could agree to devote equal time to handling some other activity around the house as a return favour.

When I started my business, I worked on it most weekends. Yes, in the beginning, it was a bit of a sacrifice. While I was working, I missed out on a few opportunities to do things with my friends that I would have enjoyed. But I was keen on becoming financially free so I did not mind sacrificing a few hours on the weekend. Simply put, I was very focused on achieving my goal and maximizing the use of my time.

USE SOME OF YOUR VACATION TIME

Here is another simple way to find time—consider setting aside a couple of vacation days to devote to your business. A good use for this time would be to attend a seminar or a workshop that is relevant to your business. And if a day or two seems a lot right now, just keep that reward in mind: financial freedom. Wouldn't it be worthwhile to use a little of your "free time" to help you win this prize at the end of the journey?

Remember—when you are financially free you can use your time anyway you want. The sacrifice is only temporary.

5

"BUT... I DON'T KNOW ENOUGH."

What and Who You Need to Know to Start Your Own Business

"I would like to start my own business but I don't have enough knowledge." Have you heard this before? Have you been using this excuse to put off starting your own business? In my circle of non-investor colleagues, I hear this all the time. People express the desire to start their own business, but they may not know enough about the field they're interested in or even where to start. There's a very easy solution to this—educate yourself! I really cannot stress this enough—education is one of the most important investments you can make for your own future and for financial freedom. In this chapter, I will show you the ways in which you can gain valuable knowledge in order to start your own business.

MY OWN EXPERIENCE

Let me share with you an example from my own experience. I am now a property investor, and I started investing in 2008. Before that, I had absolutely no knowledge about property investing whatsoever. Remember, my university degree was in biology and genetics. Until 2008, my only exposure to the world of property had been the contact I had with estate agents when I bought my own home. I was a complete novice. When I decided that I wanted to invest in property, my first thought was that I needed to educate myself otherwise I might make mistakes that I would regret.

When I first got the idea about property investing, there just so happened to be a big property expo in my city. A lot of the key names in UK investing were going to be there, and so I decided that I would go and see what was being offered. As it turned out, it was a very important day in laying the foundation of my business. I bought a book on property investing, spoke to a few other investors and attended a few free seminars. I am very glad that I made the decision to attend that expo because it gave me great insight as to how to start investing in property.

GOOGLE IT!

We are so fortunate that we can find just about anything we want by surfing the internet. This is the easiest step to take when you are looking for information that will help get your business started. It is quick, simple and absolutely free. Simply "google it" to find out what is available in terms of books, educational seminars, courses and the like to educate yourself in your chosen field.

You should also consider going to YouTube because there are often recorded professional seminars there that you can take advantage of. There are plenty of them in the field of property, and I often spend an hour in the evening listening to them. I treat each one as a live seminar, so I have my notebook in front of me and take notes. From each of these seminars, I gain some new information. They are absolutely free; all that is required is some pre-planning and the input of your time.

SEMINARS

Find professional seminars that are run in your area. Look for topics that are not only about your particular field of business, but are also about general business management or personal development. I will make a note here about seminars on personal development. These seminars were very important to me in adapting a mindset for success; they were crucial to the flourishing of my business. I actually try to balance my education time equally between property investing and developing a mindset for success. For more on the importance of having the right mindset, which I believe to be absolutely fundamental to your success, please see Chapter 9 of this book, entitled "Right Thinking."

READ, READ, READ!

Instead of picking up a trashy novel or magazine that is not going to give you any valuable information to put into your business, why don't you pick up a book that will? When I started my business, one of the first things I did was to order a number of books that were highly recommended by other successful property investors. I found these books to be excellent resources of information.

When you are finished reading this chapter, go to my website, www. TheEntrepreneurWithinBook.com, and click on Bonus 1. Here you will find a list of books that helped me tremendously in building my business.

THE POWER OF NETWORKING

Whatever business you are going to be in, you will always need a network of people around to help you. You cannot build a business on your own, however capable and skilled you are. Strong businesses are built by the work of teams of people who complement each other.

In building my own property investment business, it was very important that I had a team of people around me who could perform the tasks I could not do myself—a mortgage broker, a legal team, a good letting (leasing) agent, as well as a team of skilled tradespeople: plumber, builder, electrician, etc. I would not have been able to achieve my goals without collaborating with these people.

Do not try to work in an area that is outside your own skill set. I see a lot of people flounder because they try to fill every vacant position in their own business, even the ones that they are not good at. If the thought of doing your own accounting fills you with dread or boredom, delegate this job to an accountant. The chances are that he or she will do a much better job than you ever could, and you'll probably save money on your tax return in the long run! So, find what you are good at—whether it is managing, marketing or negotiating—and concentrate on that. For anything else, delegate, but make sure that you delegate to the right person, an expert in his or her own field.

Where do you find these people? Networking events are excellent places to find the right people to work with. You can easily find these events by searching the internet. I make a point of attending networking events in my area once or twice a month. At a networking event, you will meet other people who are in the same area of business. It is a good venue, not only for exchanging your ideas, your challenges and your ways of conducting business, but also for meeting people who handle other services that are necessary for your business. I cannot stress how important it is to surround yourself with a great team. By going through this process, you will be able to build that team.

SOCIAL MEDIA AND WEBINARS

There are a number of forums and networking groups you can join on social media, where you can post a question to a group and get an answer. These networking groups often organise webinars that are extremely valuable in keeping up to date with what is happening in your field. Most of these are either free or offered at a very low price.

TAILORED COURSES

There are professional courses you can take to learn the fundamentals of starting a business. There are a number of day and weekend courses available. When I was starting out, I attended some to gain further knowledge on particular aspects of my business. These courses are generally fee based.

Now, I often hear from beginners, "But I don't have thousands of pounds to spend on a course." Well, we have covered the "I have no money" excuse in Chapter 3. Any money you invest in your own education is the best investment you could possibly make. If you knew that in a year's time you could be making £50,000 per year from your business, would you be willing to invest £5,000 on a course? I hope your answer would be, "Of course I would!" Believe in yourself—have confidence that any money you invest in your education will be returned to you tenfold or more.

MENTORS

I would not be at this stage in my business if I had not worked with mentors at every step of the way. These are individuals who have been in my line of business for a lot longer than I have been. They are several stages ahead in their own business, so they see the industry from a completely different angle.

Think back to the people who have been influential in your life and have helped you to be where you are now. These tend to be people who encouraged you to see things differently and helped you to grow in new ways. Such people may have included a teacher, a colleague or a friend. Can you think of who they were? Can you think of someone like them who you might be able to reach out to?

When looking for a mentor, it is important to find someone who is working at a level that is higher and much more complex than the level you are working at. A "good mate" is exactly that—not someone who is your mentor! He or she will not be able to see beyond your own mental limits, so you need to find someone who can. You will find that business networking events and seminars for self-improvement are good places to seek a mentor.

You can always benefit from a mentor, especially when you are working with something that's new. Without one, you may be limiting yourself without even realising it. That's because you can only see the world from your own perspective. A mentor can broaden your horizon, help give you new perspectives and take you out of your comfort zone. So it is crucial to have a mentor to guide your growth, both personally and professionally.

In conclusion, I have given you ideas to help you gain knowledge and move your business forward. I have shown you the importance of education, in terms practical business matters and in the area of personal development. Remember—your education doesn't stop when you finish school. School only offers you some fundamentals. Educating yourself is truly a lifelong process and is essential if you wish to be successful.

I urge you to go to my website now—www.TheEntrepreneurWithinBook. com —and click on Bonus 1. Jump-start your education today!

6

"BUT ... WHAT WILL EVERYONE THINK?"

How to Move Past the Fear of Criticism

What will my family think? What will my partner think? What will my friends think? What will everyone think? These are all questions that might be going through your mind. Believe me, you're not the only one out there who has these thoughts. Are these questions stopping you from doing what you really want? Are they keeping you in a job where you can't actually see a future, where you may be doing something that you don't particularly enjoy doing? Are these questions preventing you from starting your own business?

INVOLVING FRIENDS AND FAMILY (OR NOT!)

I had similar questions going through my mind when I first started my property business. In particular, I was worried about what my family might think. Throughout my career, whenever I had expressed an interest in pursuing different earning opportunities, I was confronted with comments such as, "Well, you can't leave your job." Like most people, my family thought conventionally and perceived a job as a stable source of income and "frankly, the right thing to do." They frowned upon the idea that I might do something that would compromise my so-called secure job. The fear of their criticism weighed heavily on my mind.

I also considered what my friends would think, because a lot of them were on the same career path that I was. They had steady jobs, and so did I. Most were in respectable professions, and there I was, talking about investing in property—in a declining market.

In the beginning, I was very enthusiastic about my property business and so I spoke openly about it. This was back in 2008 when the property market in the UK was crashing. Friends confronted me with comments such as: "Are you crazy?" "Property prices are falling—why are you going into that business now?" "You don't know the first thing about property." And as for family, I knew they had my best interests at heart, but I sensed they might be overprotective and would try to dissuade me from following my intended path.

It was disappointing to experience a lack of support for something that I felt so passionate about. I quickly realised that I'd need a strategy to counteract the negative feedback. First, I remained headstrong—determined to move forward on my chosen path and build my portfolio. And then I made the decision to stop talking about my property business with my friends and family. I was not going to talk about what I was doing until I had proven to myself that I could actually be successful in this field.

A few years down the line, I am now somewhat less reserved in talking about my business plans. If I am asked, I say, "Yes, I have a property portfolio. It's going very well." Most acquaintances have been rather surprised to find out that I did not abandon my plans back in the dark days of 2008. The bottom line is that you will have to decide if you are going to talk to family and friends about your business plans. My recommendation is to be selective about who you are going to bring into your inner circle.

If you are living with a partner, then it is important that he or she understands what you are trying to accomplish. It will be difficult if you want to start you own business and your life partner is not in agreement with your plans. I would suggest taking him or her along to a networking event so that you could alleviate any fears. Perhaps your partner could get involved in the business. You might suggest an area where he or she is more capable than you might be. For example, if one of you likes to see the big picture and is very good at planning and the other is very attentive to details, you might make a very good team; the combination of your skills would be quite complementary. Actively involving your partner could be a very positive step for your business and might help you win his or her support more easily.

As for the rest of your family—your uncles, aunts and cousins—at the end of the day, do you really care what they think? When you feel strongly that the business you are pursuing will one day make you very successful, do you really want to take to heart the opinions of those who think otherwise?

PREPARE FOR TOUGH DECISIONS

I'd like to mention something that you may experience that could involve a tough decision. When you realise that a 9 to 5 J.O.B. is no longer for you, and you start making changes to break out of that mould, some people may resent you. People like to be surrounded by those who are either similar to them—in ways such as how they think or earn a living—or those who are slightly worse off than they are—so that they can feel better about themselves. Think of the saying "Birds of a feather flock together." Well, you are aspiring to become part of a different, more affluent flock. People may actually become a bit put out in seeing you become very successful. They may be bitter or jealous of your independent spirit and the fact that you are acting under your own steam; they may resent you for leaving the flock. It is not a nice trait to recognise in those we are close to, and it's unfortunate. Just be aware that this can happen, and be prepared as to how you might handle it.

You may ask, "So what would I do in this situation?" Let me share my personal experience. I had to make some difficult decisions. Simply put, I had to leave behind friends that resented my business plans and the changes I was making in my life. Since they were not supportive of what I had decided to do, in essence, they were no longer friends. I wanted to move my life in a different direction, and so I made a conscious choice to remove myself from relationships that were no longer productive or positive. So, be prepared to make some tough decisions.

SURROUND YOURSELF WITH LIKE-MINDED PEOPLE

To remove myself from an environment of negativity and criticism, I chose to mingle in different circles. One of the most important things I did was join a mentorship group. It allowed me to spend time with people who thought like I did, and I relished it. It was very refreshing to be amongst property investors who thought that this business was the best thing that they had ever been involved in. They only had positive things to say about it, and I could see plenty of evidence that they had done very well for themselves. There was no negativity whatsoever. As a member of this group, I was encouraged. Everyone was extremely helpful and wanted to see me succeed. When you surround yourself with like-minded people, you will be amongst those who will guide you, helping you to stay on course and redirecting you should you go astray.

To me, collaborating with like-minded people has been absolutely priceless. It has been worth the sacrifice of leaving part of my old social network behind. Whatever area your business is in, try to find networks of like-minded people. You will discover that members in these groups are refreshing to be around. Contrary to stereotypes that may exist, they are neither arrogant nor pretentious; they are there to help you. If you approach them in the right way, you are sure to be supported and to gain invaluable advice.

FIND MENTORS

In the previous chapter I told you that mentors are a great resource for obtaining the knowledge you need to move forward with your business. They can also be a great source of support and inspiration.

Life is always a little easier when you have someone around to help you. If you are just starting your business, you need someone who is working at a much higher level in the business than you are. Make this type of person your mentor. This individual will most likely have had experience in dealing with the negativity that entrepreneurs often face. Let this person share his or her experiences, and you may soon find yourself operating at a whole new level. Mentors will help you deal with the lack of support you may find yourself surrounded by when you first start your business—and beyond.

GROW A "THICK SKIN"

I say this half-jokingly as I end this chapter, but growing an extra thick skin can really help. It did for me. After a while, I realised that other people's opinions of me and what I was doing did not matter. I had set a new course for my life. I had dreams. I had ideas about what I wanted to achieve in my life. And I had goals. Whether other people agreed with them or not was no longer important. Instead, my goals became what was most important. So, learn to grow a thick skin! Set yourself some ambitious goals, take action and realise your dreams. After a while, you won't even hear negative comments anymore.

7

"BUT ... WHAT IF I FAIL?"

How to Eliminate the Fear of Failure

What if I fail? Is this one of the questions that goes through your head when you think about starting your own business? You know you have some good ideas but there always seems to be this little voice saying, "Don't do it—you are going to fail." Fear of failure is a very common fear that prevents people from getting to their perfect place in life. In this chapter, I will show you ways to move past the fear, and help you get your business moving forward.

ASSESSING RISK

Where does your fear of failure come from? Your insecurity? Your logical nature? A convincing voice in your head? Perhaps it's the idea of taking a risk that makes you think that you're going to fail. To address this issue, you should consider what level of risk you'd find acceptable and assess the types of risk that you'd be taking by starting your own business.

Risk is around us everywhere. Every morning when you wake up, you are going to face some risks—by driving your car, by crossing the road, by travelling to work, by plugging your computer into the socket. We face risks all the time, and they never stop us from doing what we'd normally do. We still drive our cars and walk across busy roads—we carry on with our lives even though we know there are risks—and we don't fear that we might become victims by taking these risks. To do otherwise would allow fear to rule our lives, which would be a terrible way to live. So what would you accept as a reasonable level of risk? There are some risks that you can't control, such as freak accidents, but for many, you are in complete control.

What are the types of risk that you would be taking by starting your own business? Well, eventually you would be leaving your current job. For most of us a job means security—it means a fixed amount of money every month. But think about this. Isn't there a risk that you might one day be laid off, especially in the current climate? Or what if your company goes out of business? Lifetime employment is not guaranteed. What risks are you running by actually staying in your job? How about the risk of giving an employer most of your life and receiving a pension that may be inadequate? Isn't this a risk that you are running?

So with your business, yes, you are running a risk, but you are in control of the level and types of risk that you'd be comfortable with. This is the secret—it's a very calculated, knowledgeable risk.

EMPOWERING ACTIONS

If you keep asking yourself, "What if I fail?" this is exactly what you're focusing on—failure. This is not an empowering question. It puts you in a position of weakness rather than strength. Instead of focusing on failure, focus on success. It would be much more powerful to say, "What do I need to do in order to succeed in my business?" Having the right mindset is very important. While I will more fully address this topic in Chapter 9, for now I will simply state that our minds are powerful—always fill yours with strong, positive thoughts.

Make a list of all the things you need to do in terms of getting the right skills, working with the right people, and focusing on the right business area. What do you need to do to be successful? Write it down! You will find that when you start writing things in a logical manner, you will actually create ways to minimise risks. When you see your business plan written down, complete with the action steps that you will be taking to make the business succeed, the thoughts of failure will soon dissipate.

Don't be fearful about making mistakes. Everybody makes them, and you can use them as learning experiences. Don't beat yourself up about them because again, that is not a powerful position to be in. Look at the situation, see what you've learned, and move on. Taking this approach is empowering. I can assure you that every successful person has made mistakes, and wouldn't have reached his or her level of achievement without having pushed through them.

In Bonus 1 (www.TheEntrepreneurWithinBook.com), I have listed some reading material that will help you cultivate positive thoughts and find antidotes for your fear of failure.

You now have the tools to handle the fear of failure excuse. So if you should hear a voice in your head saying, "What if I fail?" stop it right there! Remember, you are in control of the voice because that voice is YOU. Make your voice, your thoughts and your actions work with you, not against you, and you will have a whole new way of looking at things—with a lot less fear.

8
GETTING DOWN TO BUSINESS
A Guide to Help You Get Started

In this chapter I provide a step-by-step guide to help you start your own business. I must admit that I was a lot more haphazard in my approach to getting started. I didn't do things in quite the right order, so I wanted to make life a lot easier for you. Before I go over the detailed steps, I want to address two "big picture" elements.

CHOOSE YOUR TYPE OF BUSINESS

Since the subject of this book intrigued you enough to purchase it, you probably already have an idea of the type of business you'd like to start. Whether you do or you don't, I have one strong recommendation. Make sure it involves something that's in an area of extreme interest to you—something that you love to do. Ask yourself: "What are my passions?" What is it that gets you out of bed in the morning and makes you feel alive? Indentify your true passion.

If you look at all the truly successful people in the world, you'll find that they are doing what they love. If you select a business that does not makes you tick, chances are that you will soon get frustrated, discouraged and lose total interest. Simply put, if you don't love what you're doing, it will hurt your chances for success.

WRITE DOWN YOUR GOALS

This is very important. What do you want to achieve financially? Write down what you want to achieve in your first six months in business. Write down what you want to achieve in the first year, and then where you see yourself in five years' time. It is very important that you have a clear idea of where you want your business to go—how big you want it to be. Not only will these goals be essential to your business plan, but they will help you stay on track and measure your progress. Remember, if you don't know where you are heading, how will you reach your destination?

I have prepared a chart to help you record your goals and track your progress. When you are done with this chapter, visit my website, www. TheEntrepreneurWithinBook.com, and click on Bonus 4.

Personal development goals are just as important as your business goals. You need to have those in order to drive you forward. It's very important for you to grow both professionally and personally, so write down where you want to be in six months' time, in a year's time and in five years' time in terms of your own personal development.

THE STEP-WISE GUIDE

Once you've chosen your field of interest and identified some big picture goals, it's time to get down to the details. Each step below is presented in a logical order to help get your business started. While you may feel that it will take a big leap to go from where you are now to actually being in business, that's not necessarily so. Each step is very small, and more importantly, each step is very, very doable. Even if you were to tackle one step every few days, you would quickly get to the point of having your business up and running.

STEP 1: CHOOSE A NAME FOR YOUR BUSINESS

Make this memorable or catchy, something that, when people see your business card, they will remember who you are and what you do. Needless to say, make this all relevant to your business.

STEP 2: IDENTIFY YOUR MARKET

Who will you serve, and where will you do business? Identify the type of people you are going to be doing business with, and find the right geographical area in which you are going to operate. For a business like property investing, you might have to drive around to get a feel for the areas in which you should be buying. Look for the good areas in terms of rental income and eliminate areas that are probably too expensive to invest in.

STEP 3: CREATE A BUSINESS PLAN

If you are going to be asking anyone to lend you money, you will need to write a business plan. This would include a description of the business (your product and intended market), and financial features (projected sales, profits, capital needed to start the business, etc.). When I started in property investing, my business plan identified what type of properties I was going to concentrate on and which areas would work best for me. I also determined how much profit I would be looking for from each deal. There are many excellent resources in print and on-line that you can find to help you write the perfect plan.

STEP 4: SPEAK TO YOUR BANK MANAGER

Your bank manager can be your friend. Based on your business plan, he or she will tell you how much money you can borrow—from a bank or from the equity in your home. This will be your source of seed capital. It will get you started for the first few months. By the end of this step, you will know how much capital you will have to get started.

STEP 5: OPEN A BUSINESS BANK ACCOUNT

Open a business bank account even if you don't have anything to put in it. It impresses upon your mind that you're actually going to start a business. It also shows a commitment to moving forward. It will feel great to have that bank account already available when your business starts earning money.

STEP 6: GET YOUR BUSINESS CARDS PRINTED

This does not need to be an expensive endeavour. I made my own first set of business cards from an on-line company, and they only cost me £5. Once you have your cards in hand, your business will start feeling very real.

STEP 7: START EDUCATING YOURSELF

Now's the time to put aside that novel, no matter how gripping, and turn off the TV. Instead of investing hours in those activities, spend some time reading books that show you how to develop a business, and in particular, those written on the topic of your business. When I started working in the property investment field, I was trying to finish a book every week on this subject.

STEP 8: START NETWORKING

Look out for networking events in your area and attend as many as you can. Give out your business cards, and make sure that you take cards from others. Get to know the members. Don't be scared to ask them questions; you'd be surprised how much people will want to help you.

If your type of business will require associates, use networking events to find them. In property investing, I work with tradespeople like plumbers, electricians and builders. Networking will not only help you learn more about your field, but it will also be a great resource for team building.

STEP 9: CREATE YOUR WEBSITE

Your business will dictate the complexity of your website. Your website could just be there for status purposes, simply to give you visibility. Obviously, if you are going to start an internet marketing business, your website will be your marketing and sales tool. Decide on the purpose of your website and start designing it, either by yourself or with the help of a professional.

STEP 10: IDENTIFY THE BEST WAY TO MARKET YOURSELF

This could be through your website, a newspaper ad or leaflets. Decide what will be the best way to reach your target market. You may want to start locally and expand your geographical area as your business grows.

STEP 11: START MARKETING!

Once you've determined what the best approach will be, get going! Give people your business card, distribute leaflets or get your website live. Whatever it is, spread the word that you're actually now "open for business."

STEP 12: WELCOME YOUR FIRST CLIENT!

Stick to your business plan and don't get carried away by emotions. You're on your way to success!

Even if you run into some bumps along the road, keep moving forward. If some aspect of your business plan is not working, don't be disheartened—just make a change. Believe in yourself, focus on your goals and trust me, your first client will come. The most important step is … to take the first step.

9
RIGHT THINKING
Developing the Right Mindset

When I first started my property business, I went to a property seminar, and I will never forget one particular statement that I heard. The presenter said, "If you want to be successful in your business, it is 20 percent knowledge and 80 percent mindset." That got me to question my own mindset. Until that point, I thought that in order to start a business you simply had to learn as much as you could about your particular line of work. I thought that if I read books about my field of interest, went to seminars and learned as much as I could, my business would be successful. In other words, the best approach was to cram in as much knowledge as possible—isn't that what they taught you at school? Well, I couldn't have been more wrong. Remember this fact: 20 percent knowledge and 80 percent mindset. Yes, the right mindset is truly that critical. From that moment on, I spent as much time cultivating the right mindset as I did learning about issues directly related to my business.

In reality, financially free people don't think the same way as "poor people." When I say "poor people," I refer to those who rely on a 9 to 5 J.O.B to make ends meet—in other words, the majority of the population. Could you ever envision the likes of Donald Trump or Richard

Branson getting up in the morning, working 9 to 5, coming back home, sitting on the sofa and watching TV? Is that the lifestyle that you think they have? The mere thought is laughable. Do you think they are afraid of trying something new and venturing somewhere they've never been before? No, certainly not—otherwise they wouldn't be Donald Trump or Richard Branson. They think very, very differently from the way most other people think; they have the right mindset. This doesn't happen overnight. To get the right mindset, you have to start eliminating what I call "limiting beliefs." These are ones that are keeping you where you are right now.

In this chapter, I am going to show you ways to develop the right mindset, replacing limiting beliefs with those that will empower you and push you beyond the boundaries of your comfort zone, so that you will have the mindset for success.

READ THE RIGHT BOOKS

There are numerous books out there that will help you develop the mindset for success. Personal development books were keenly instrumental in developing mine. They challenged me. They challenged the things that I thought were set in stone. They challenged some of the basic beliefs that were instilled in me at school. They got me thinking about how poor people act and think and how rich people act and think. I was absolutely changed by books of this nature. Not only will personal development books help change your mindset, but they will ultimately change your life. They will be fundamental to the success of your business. Once you have finished reading this chapter, I encourage you to go to my website, www.TheEntrepreneurWithinBook.com, where I have listed some of these important books in Bonus 1. I really encourage you to get some of them in your hands as soon as possible.

GO TO PERSONAL DEVELOPMENT SEMINARS

If you live in the UK, USA or Australasia, you are very fortunate because seminars for personal development are given on a regular basis. These are as fundamental as reading books in instilling new principles for success. To find these types of events, all you need to do is google "personal development" or "entrepreneur skills." These seminars also have a secondary benefit; they are also tremendous networking events. After attending these events, you will gradually see yourself transforming.

ELIMINATE THE NEGATIVE

For me, this was one of the most challenging aspects in developing a new mindset. I realised that if I was going to be successful, I had to get rid of all the sources of negativity in my life—be they friends, hobbies or habits.

Surely you must know someone in your network of acquaintances that just sucks all the energy out of you. Do you know the type of person I mean? The person who whines and complains about everything and always talks about all the terrible things that are happening; the person who gets infected by every virus or disease that is going around; the person who always sees the glass half empty and never half full. You must know this type of person. Well, this is my advice—get rid of that person, because otherwise, his or her negativity will rub off on you! It might seem cruel to you right now, but if you want to be successful, then you must find a way to gradually remove people like this from your life. The right mindset leaves no room for negativity, only positive, empowering thoughts; no room for giving up, only trying again and again; no room for failure, only successful outcomes.

You also need to look at your own negative habits, those that are stopping you from moving forward. If you want to be successful in your business, you will have to change your lifestyle. The majority of people will stay in the same place all their lives because they refuse to make any changes. They will say, "You can't teach an old dog new tricks." Well, guess what? You can. But YOU, the "old dog," will have to want to be taught "new tricks." If you are someone who spends two to three hours a night watching TV, what could you do differently in that time? Is it possible that you could do some business planning? Could you read some useful books? Could you start looking at ways to become financially free? Break the habits that are holding you back and do something inspired.

ACCENT THE POSITIVE

If you want to be successful, you absolutely need to surround yourself with positive, successful people. In doing so, you will actually become like those people. I learned that in terms of your finances, your behaviour and your success, you will represent the average of the five people you most associate with. It is a great truth.

Earlier in this book I mentioned the importance of networking events. You can easily find positive, successful people at these venues. I still recall how daunting my first property networking event was. I was headed toward a room full of people that I didn't know, and in my mind, they all seemed extremely successful—extremely confident. I imagined them as all being millionaires, knowing exactly what they were doing. As I put one foot through the door, I had second thoughts. But something inside me said, "Come on, get yourself in to see what this is all about." By the end of the evening I realised that people from all walks of life had attended. They included people like me, who had just started on a journey in property investing and were there to learn. Of course there were people there who had been investing in property for years, those with respectable property portfolios. They were there because they were still learning, too. And yes, there were millionaires there. They were still networking with people, even people like me! What amazed me was that no one was arrogant, no one was unfriendly, and no one looked down on me. Every time I asked someone a question, I was greeted with a polite response—everyone was happy to help me. I was really pleased that I managed to find the courage to walk through that door and experience my first property networking event. Spending time with positive, successful people enhanced my mindset and paved a path to help me move forward with confidence.

DEVELOP THE RIGHT PERSONAL QUALITIES

I have often been asked "What are the right personal qualities needed to start your own business?" While there are many qualities that are desirable, I have found the following three to be absolutely essential:

1. **Perseverance.** In my opinion, the ability to be persistent is the most important trait to have. It's an integral part of the mindset of any successful person. How many times are you going to try before you succeed? 10? 20? 1000? My answer to that is that if you want to achieve your dreams, you will have to try until you succeed. Yes, keep trying. If you are the type of person

who gives up after a couple of unsuccessful attempts, you can do one of two things: either change your attitude and learn to keep trying, or accept the fact that the 9 to 5 J.O.B. is going to be your best option in life.

2. **Seeing opportunities and taking action.** Most people—I would say 90 percent of the population—when put in front of a good opportunity wouldn't even know it was a good one. That's because they haven't been conditioned to look for one. Another 3 to 4 percent of the population will see an opportunity, believe it is a good one and then ignore their gut instinct. Why? Well, they may hear that little voice in their head saying, "You can't do this—it's too risky." Or they may be influenced by their friends' opinions. Their friends are likely to be entirely ignorant about the subject and so their advice would be, "Don't be so stupid—stick to your safe job." Another 3 to 4 percent will look at a good opportunity, recognise it is a good one, and then procrastinate. They will simply let a great idea slip away.

It is vital to learn how to recognise an opportunity, stick to your guns and take action. The reality is that only about 2 percent of the population will follow this course—and that 2 percent will become financially free. When you think about it, all they are up against is other peoples' ignorance and procrastination.

3. **Rigorous self-discipline.** I have mentioned this enough times in this book—if you want to achieve the dream of being financially free, you will have to make changes in your life—your habits, your friends and your lifestyle. To do this, you will need to develop self-discipline. All the successful people I know use

their time very efficiently. If you are someone who is perpetually putting things off until tomorrow, you can do one of two things: either set a new daily regime that allows you two to three hours per day to devote to your business, or accept that you are better suited to a 9 to 5 J.O.B.

If you do not want to do the things needed to develop the right mindset, just remember—your current lifestyle and your current belief system have brought you to where you are now.

Yes, there may be challenges in starting your own business. You may have to demand things from yourself beyond what you thought could be possible. But the rewards at the end are well worth that journey. So, it is now time to look at what some of these rewards could be.

10

THE REWARDS
Creating a New Life

In this final chapter, I want to explore some fundamental questions. The first one is: "Why do you want to start your own business?" What is your reason for wanting to be in business? Do you want to have more creativity in your life? Do you simply dislike your current job and want to part company with your boss? Do you want to use your wealth to help others? Do you want to leave your family a large inheritance? Whatever your reason may be, write it down. This must be the driving force in your life. If it is not powerful enough, you will run out of fuel half way through the journey.

The second question is: "Why do you want to be financially free?" What are you going to do with your financial freedom? Do you want more free time so that you can pursue activities you enjoy? Do you want to spend your time going on luxury holidays? Do you want a big home or an expensive car? Do you want a secure retirement? Do you want to leave a legacy for your children? Again, if you do not have a clear answer to this question, you are chasing an empty dream—one that will not materalise. Write down your reason.

I am asking you to write down these reasons because they are going to propel you forward to do something different with your life. It is very likely that unless you have answered "the why," you are probably never going to do anything that I have said in this book. So identify your own personal "why."

To help with this process, I want you to create a chart entitled "My Life In 10 Years' Time." So, get out a piece of paper, and divide it into two columns. At the top of the column on the left-hand side, write "If I Do Nothing." Write down exactly where you believe you will be in 10 years' time if your life stays as it is right now. Write down your expected salary. Write down what you think your health will be like. Write down what you think you will be doing with your free time. Write down where you believe you will be living. Write down what you feel you will be aspiring to do.

At the top of the column on the right-hand side, write "When I Become Financially Free." Assume that you now have all the money in the world, and let your imagination flow. What income will you have? Where will you be living? What special things will you have around you? What kind of holidays will you be taking? Where will you be with your life, both personally and professionally? Just imagine what your life would be like in 10 years' time if you were financially free. Write it all down.

MY LIFE IN 10 YEARS' TIME	
If I Do Nothing	**When I Become Financially Free**
My income:	My income:
My house:	My house:
My car:	My car:
My pension:	My pension:
My free time:	My free time:
My holiday:	My holiday:

These lists are representative of areas in which you may experience life changes and are not exhaustive. You are encouraged to customize your lists as appropriate to your circumstance.

Now compare the two lists. On which side would you like to be? Does this give you a big why? Does this give you a good reason to start your own business? Aren't the rewards worth pursuing?

You can go to my website, www.TheEntrepreneur WithinBook.com, and click on Bonus 5 to download a PDF of this form so that you can customise it to suit your circumstances.

What I have shared with you in this book is the principle that starting your own business is actually simple. Don't get me wrong—it is not effortless. Nothing worthwhile comes without effort, otherwise everyone would be a millionaire. The steps I have presented are simple enough that anyone can follow them—if he or she chooses to do so. By changing some fundamental ways of thinking, by taking action, by stepping over a few hurdles and by persevering—by not giving up in the face of challenges—you can do it.

As encouragement, I would like you to know that I am no longer 100% reliant on the "security" of a 9 to 5 J.O.B. for my income. I have built an investment property portfolio valued at over £1 million. Remember, there was nothing extraordinary about my beginnings. I have begun to reap the rewards of starting my own business and creating a new life. If I can do it, you can do it. You can do something extraordinary.

I wish you success on your journey to financial freedom. Enjoy the ride!

19240418R00041

Made in the USA
Charleston, SC
13 May 2013